SAME HERE!

THE DIFFERENCES WE SHARE

Written by
SUSAN HUGHES

Illustrated by
SOPHIE CASSON

Owlkids Books

What if children from all around the world met to share stories about their lives? Would they discover many differences? Would they have anything in common?

Certainly, the lives of children around the world are different in many ways—the languages they speak, the families they belong to, the homes they live in, and the chores they do. Depending on where they live, they might have different favorite foods, favorite subjects at school, favorite ways to have fun. Their dreams for the future would probably be different, too!

But they all have something that unites them, no matter where they grow up: they share the same needs—**we all do!**

We All Need to Communicate

WHAT WERE YOUR FIRST WORDS?

United States

Si!
Dah woozh!
Hi!

Hello! I'm Erica, and I love to talk. Sometimes Mom and Dad say they should have named me Chatterbox!

I said my first words before I was even one year old. They were *dah woozh*, *si*, and "hi." *Dah woozh* is how you say "strawberry" in Navajo. My mom is a member of the Navajo Nation and grew up speaking both Navajo and English. *Si* is how you say "yes" in Spanish. My dad grew up speaking Spanish and English in his family. And I said "hi" because Mom and Dad speak English to me, too!

So I know words in *three* languages. **I love how words connect me to my family and our history!**

Uganda

"ball"

Same here! I know lots of words in Ugandan Sign Language and English. But my very first word was "ball."

Hola! I speak Spanish. My first words were *mamá*, which means "mother," and *mío*, which means "mine."

Colombia

Bonjour! I speak French and English. My first word was *nounours*. That's "teddy bear" in French.

New Caledonia

Egypt

Assalamu alaikum! I speak Arabic. My first word was *baba*. That means "dad."

← me, when I was a baby

Nǐ hǎo! That means "hello" in Mandarin, but I also speak Malay and English. My first word was in Malay. I said *tidak*, which means "no."

Malaysia

Boozhoo! I speak Ojibwe and English. My first word in Ojibwe was *nookomis*. That's "grandmother."
What was YOUR first word?

Canada

We All Need to Feel Loved and Protected

WHAT'S YOUR FAMILY LIKE?

Hello! My name is Ochieng, and I live with my older brother and sister, my mother and father, my grandfather, and Mercy. Mercy's mom and mine were best friends. Mercy became part of our family when her parents died.

My grandfather tells us stories before we go to sleep. He was a photojournalist, and we love hearing about his real-life adventures. He also tells stories about the village he lived in long ago. Sometimes he even tells us funny stories about our moms.

I know Mercy still really misses her mom and dad, but Grandpa's stories always make her laugh. ***Our family takes good care of us.***

Kenya

Same here! Both my dads work from home, so they take turns walking my sister and me to school. Some days we all go together.

Canada

Me, too! I have a huge extended family. Some of my relatives live in a city, but many of us live here in our village. We look out for one another, sharing food and work—and fun times!

Mozambique

Turkey

When the town near our farm was bombed, we had to flee. My aunt and uncle welcomed us with hugs. "Our home is your home," they said.

Papua, New Guinea

I just got a new baby brother. I help take care of him. Finally, I'm not the youngest anymore!

Pakistan

I live in Pakistan, but my dad works in Saudi Arabia doing construction. He makes more money for our family there than here, but he misses us. I miss him, too. **What's YOUR family like?**

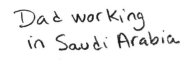

Dad working in Saudi Arabia

We All Need Shelter

WHAT DO YOU LIKE BEST ABOUT YOUR HOME?

Hello! I'm Somchai, and this is where I live. My parents built our house before I was born. My grandparents taught them how, and one day my parents will teach me.

The house has lots of windows to let in breezes when it's hot. So it's nice to be inside when we're sleeping or it's raining. But we spend most of our time outside.

Thailand

At night, we go out on our porch, where it's cool. And on hot, sunny days, we go *under* the house. The best part of our house is its stilts, which make it like a big sun umbrella. It's always shady and cool underneath. Plus, there are floods every year during the rainy season. The stilts keep the house nice and dry above the water!

All the houses where we live are designed the same way. My house may look like all the others, but it's special to me. **I love my home!**

Same here! I live high up in an apartment building. I share a room with my siblings. We love looking out our window at the sparkling city below.

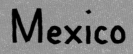

Mexico

I love my home, too! Three times a year, we move with our animals so they have fresh grass to eat. We take down our house and bring it along. Wherever we are, that's home!

Mongolia

We just moved to the third floor of an apartment building. The stairs are hard for me, but there's an elevator I can use instead.

Ukraine

I'm so glad I can take the elevator!

Tanzania

Our house is one big room. My favorite part is our new solar panel! Now I can do my homework even when it's dark outside.
What's the best thing about YOUR home?

We All Need to Learn

WHAT'S YOUR FAVORITE THING ABOUT SCHOOL?

Hi, my name is Salma. Where I live, the land all around is low. There are lots of rivers and lakes. Twice a year, it rains and rains. It feels like it will never stop! Water covers all the roads and paths, which makes it hard to go places.

But my friends and I don't have to miss school! That's because our school is a boat. It picks us up every day.

We have books and a teacher, of course. And because our boat uses solar power for electricity, we have a computer, too. It's my favorite thing. We all take turns using it and going on the internet. When it's my turn, I like to look up the latest space missions. ***Science is my favorite subject!***

Bangladesh

Same here! I love learning about science, too—especially about raising animals. Dad's teaching me lots about the goats and cows on our farm. When I have time to go to school, I learn to read, do math, and think like a scientist.

Ethiopia

I like learning about different countries and solving math problems. Most of all, I like that we play outside after every single class. Recess is the best!

Finland

My school has only girls, but we learn the same subjects as the boys. My favorite is art. I like drawing imaginary cities and futuristic machines.

Saudi Arabia

I eat at the school breakfast club every morning. I like seeing my friends before school, and now I always get a full meal before starting classes. The toasted bagels are the best!

England

me

Sam

Fadel↗

Tina

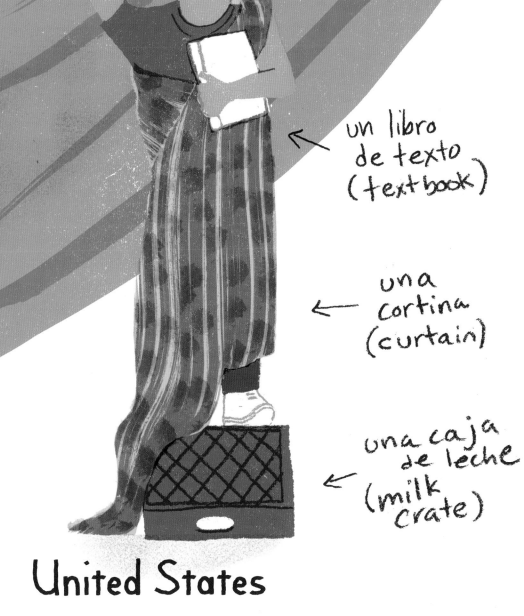

un libro
de texto
(textbook)

una
cortina
(curtain)

una caja
de leche
(milk
crate)

United States

Spanish is one of my favorite classes. But
the best thing about school is drama club.

When I'm not shining shoes,
I go to school. Both are hard work.
I'm proud of how good I'm getting at
numbers and reading. *What do YOU*
like best about school?

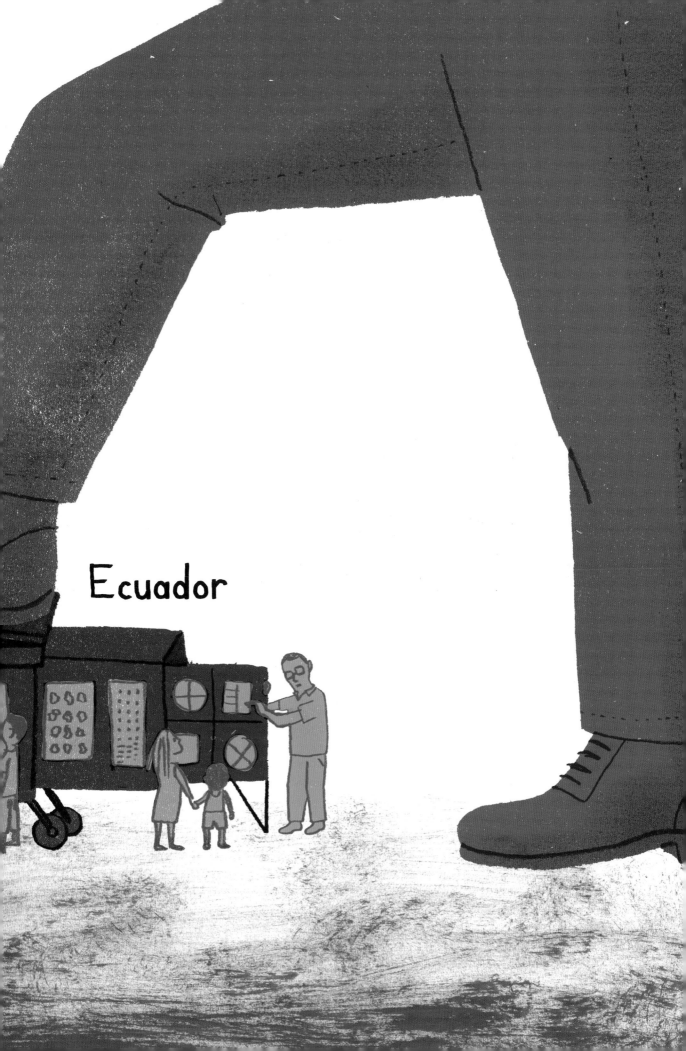

Ecuador

We All Need to Eat

WHAT'S YOUR FAVORITE MEAL?

Hi, I'm Alec. Every Saturday morning, I go with my dad to get our groceries for the week. But first, we plan our meals for the whole week and make a list of food to buy. Dad says this helps make sure we have what we need and that nothing goes to waste.

Usually, we go to the supermarket near our house. It's the biggest store I've ever seen. They have all kinds of food there, so Dad and I have a game that we play. Every week, he picks a new food for me to try, one that's not on our shopping list. Last week, it was green olives. They kind of look like grapes, but they definitely don't taste like them!

It's fun spending this time together, planning and shopping. I'm in charge of choosing Friday night dinner, and I always pick pasta! ***I love it when we have my favorite food for dinner.***

United States

Same here! For almost every meal, Mom cooks with maize flour. Most often, she cooks it into a thick porridge called *nshima*. My favorite is when she makes it like bread, to dip into *ifisashi*—peanut stew.

Zambia

Bahamas

We eat a lot of fish and seafood. But my favorite meal is a big square of gooey macaroni pie.

Mmm, cumin!

My family is vegetarian. We buy fresh vegetables at the market every day. Sometimes we buy spices, too. Mom uses them to make the tastiest dishes—like my favorite, *saag paneer*!

India

My favorite part of dinner is dessert—especially when it's *knafeh* with orange blossom syrup on top. Sometimes Dad brings it home from the bakery near his work.

pistachios (yummy!)

Jordan

South Korea

These are banchan—small side dishes.

We eat at restaurants a lot. I always order my favorite: *bulgogi* and rice. I like that it comes with lots of *banchan* and *kimchi*! **What's YOUR favorite meal?**

We All Need to Help Our Families
HOW DO YOU HELP OUT AT HOME?

Hi, I'm Tim, and my brother is Danny. We're fraternal twins, which means we don't look exactly alike. We are different in other ways, too. Danny loves drawing and walking the dog, and I love playing sports like cricket. He has Down syndrome and I don't.

We like to do things together—even our chores. We set the table, vacuum our room, and take out the garbage and recycling.

New Zealand

Also, Danny and I sing our little sister, Rose, to sleep every night. That's not really a chore, though. It's our idea to do it: we love Rose, and we love singing.

Sometimes Danny and I complain about having too many chores. But mostly, **we feel good when we help out.**

Same here! Every day, I get water for my family before and after school. I used to walk to the river, but now our village has a well.

my house ↓

Afghanistan

Singapore

My sister and I help with the
laundry. We bring in the dry clothes,
fold them, and put them away.

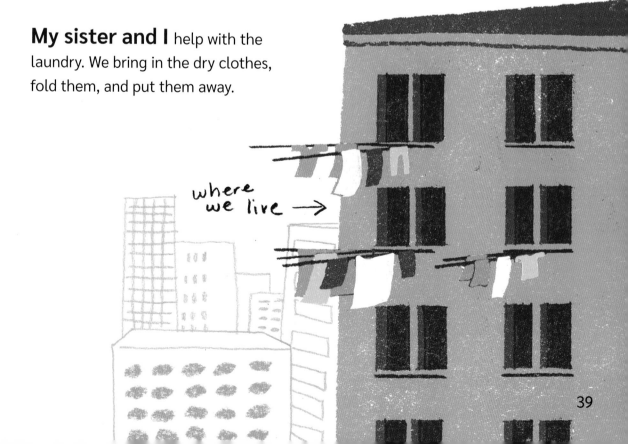

where
we live →

Every morning before school, I spend time collecting firewood for cooking. Soon, we'll get a mud stove that needs less wood. Then there'll be more time for me to help out in other ways.

Burundi

One of my chores is feeding our chickens and pigs. I always make sure the little ones get their share.

Nicaragua

I help my parents with our flower farm. We sell the flowers at the local market. On those days, I have to wake up very early. *What do YOU do to help out?*

Ireland

Some sunflowers grow tall!

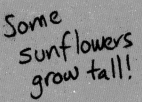

We All Need Community
HOW DO YOU HELP YOUR NEIGHBORS?

I'm Jurrien. I belong to an after-school club run by my teacher. We get to play games and work on art projects. We also talk about ways we can help others.

Our group came up with a good idea. Some of our grandparents live in a nearby retirement home, and not everyone who lives there has visitors. Now our club visits the retirement home every two weeks. Some of us bring along board games or a deck of cards. Lots of people want to play games, and it's fun for us, too. It's a good way for everyone to make new friends. ***I like helping people!***

Netherlands

43

China

Same here! I sweep my neighbor's sidewalk when it snows, and he sometimes makes steamed buns for my mom and me to say thank you.

South Africa

COMPOST

USE A REFILLABLE BOTT

Today, my class made posters about how to help the Earth. We taped them up everywhere to share our ideas.

Once a day, all the kids at my school clean the halls and classrooms. It's not much fun, but it's important for everyone to help out.

Japan

Dad and I are leading the "walking school bus" today. The neighborhood kids all walk together instead of being driven to school. It's a fun way to reduce our carbon footprint.

Canada

Graphic novels are what I like best!

Chile

I'm always borrowing books from our public library because I love to read. I volunteer there as often as I can. Mostly, I help our librarian reshelve the books.

How do you help YOUR community?

We All Need to Play

WHAT DO YOU DO FOR FUN?

My name is Adwoa, and I love cooking with my mom and playing with my friends.

Most mornings before school, I help get the food ready for our supper. It's too hot to cook later in the day. My mother is teaching me how to make a kind of dough called *fufu*. While Mom pounds plantains with water, I add peeled and boiled cassavas. Making *fufu* takes time, but now I'm getting really good at it!

Ghana

After school, my friends and I go straight home to do chores. But we always try to finish quickly so we have time to play outside before supper. *I love playing with my friends!*

Same here! I love skateboarding with my friends at the park. I like listening to music, too. Samba and hip-hop are my favorites.

Brazil

I like playing chess with my friends, but it's even more fun to play with my grandmother. I think she lets me win, but she says I'm just getting really good!

Russia

For fun, I play video games with my friends. I also like taking coding classes.

Spain

Indonesia

I like playing on computers, too, but one of my favorite things is kite flying. When my cousin comes from the city for a visit, he always brings his kite so we can fly them together.

Nothing's better than reading comic books and drawing cartoons. I show my favorite drawings to my best friend, Milo.
What do YOU do for fun?

United States

We All Need to Dream

WHAT'S YOUR DREAM FOR THE FUTURE?

Dominican Republic

Hi, I'm Catalina. If I could have any dream come true, it would be for my friend Luis to be able to go to school.

Where I live, you have to wear a special uniform and shoes to attend school. Luis's family can't afford to buy them, so he can't go.

But he and I have a plan. After school, I do my homework with Luis and show him everything we learned that day. That way, if he gets to come to school soon, he won't be behind in his studies.

I hope my dream comes true.

Same here! I dream about inventing ways to make crops grow, even when there isn't much rain.

My dream is for everyone on Earth to work together to keep the planet healthy. I really hope my dream comes true, too.

Australia

My dream is to be a famous singer. I'll tour the world! I'll earn enough money to look after my whole family.

China

I live on a riverboat. I dream of living on land in a house so I can have a dog and a cat!

Vietnam

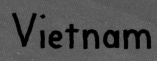

Nigeria

When I grow up, I want to help people. But I can't choose between being a doctor or a teacher! *What's YOUR dream for the future?*

FURTHER READING

Children Just Like Me: A New Celebration of Children Around the World.
New York: DK Children, 2016.

Lamothe, Matt. *This Is How We Do It: One Day in the Lives of Seven Kids from Around the World.* San Francisco: Chronicle Books, 2017.

Serres, Alain, and Aurélia Fronty. *I Have the Right to Be a Child.* Toronto: Groundwood Books, 2012.

This Is My World: Meet 84 Kids from Around the Globe. Lonely Planet Kids, 2019.

SELECTED SOURCES

Boateng, John, and Akosua Adomako Ampofo. "How Parenting in Ghana Shapes Sexist Stereotypes." *The Conversation.* Academic Journalism Society, 20 Jan. 2016. Online.

"Brazilian Skateboard Highlights." *Soul Brasil Magazine,* 17 Jul. 2017. Online.

Bungane, Babalwa. "Solar Power Dominates Rural Tanzania, Says Report." *ESI Africa,* 27 Apr. 2017. Online.

Cira, Dean. "What Will Kenya's Urban Future Look Like for Newborns James and Maureen?" *Africa Can End Poverty* (blog). The World Bank, 16 Mar. 2016. Online.

Curtis, Andrea. *What's for Lunch? How Schoolchildren Eat Around the World.* Markham, ON: Red Deer Press, 2012.

Down the Stream. Directed by Mai Huyen Chi, Aeon Video, 4 Dec. 2015. Online.

Fernandez, Isabel. "The Importance of Floating Schools." The Borgen Project, 11 Jun. 2019. Online.

Fihlani, Pumza. "Why Africa Should Stop Eating One of Its Favourite Foods." BBC News, 18 Sept. 2019. Online.

Harris, Rebecca. "Energy Access for Poverty Eradication in Burundi." The Borgen Project, 24 Oct. 2020. Online.

Hays, Jeffrey. "Homes in Thailand: Bamboo Houses, Teak Houses, Raft Homes, Condominiums and Suburban Concrete Town Houses." factsanddetails.com. Last updated May 2014. Online.

Kelly, Kevin. "What Mongolian Nomads Teach Us About the Digital Future." *Wired*. 21 Oct. 2017. Online.

"Kids Around the World." *Fact Monster*. Sandbox Networks, Inc. Last updated 21 Feb. 2017. Online.

Levine, Jon. "Kids in Japan Are Doing Something Incredible That the U.S. Should Consider." *Mic*. BDG Media Inc., 12 May 2016. Online.

MobileSchool.org. Online.

Ng, Jane. "Taking the Chore Out of Housework During the Holidays." *The Strait Times*, 20 Jun. 2016. Online.

"Over 87% of Pakistani Migrant Workers Headed for UAE, Saudi Arabia in 2019." *Middle East Monitor*. 10 Aug. 2020. Online.

"Photo Kit: A Day in the Life of 5 Children." *World Vision*. World Vision Australia, 2013. Online.

Prisk, Cath "Playtime Matters Report." *Outdoor Classroom Day*. Semble, 28 Apr. 2019. Online.

Rees-Bloor, Natasha. "Schools Around the World—in Pictures." *The Guardian*, 2 Oct. 2015. Online.

"Robots and Computational Thinking at Mn. Albert Vives School in Spain." EU Code Week Blog, 14 Dec. 2018. Online.

UNICEF MENA and EU. *The Book of Dreams*. UNICEF, November 2019. Online.

USAID Water Team. "Upgrading Rural Afghanistan's Water Supply." Global Waters, 26 Jan. 2018. Online.

"Walking School Bus." Ecology Action Centre website, 2020. Online.

For all the children
—S.H.

I dedicate these images to the
children who inspire me every day
with their openness to the world:
my sons and my partner's daughters
—S.C.

ACKNOWLEDGMENTS

With thanks to the following people and organizations for their help: Verónica Abud, Fundación la Fuente, Chile; Anishinaabemodaa—Waking Up Ojibwe, Canada; Javi Cubillos, Cuba; Shazia Fazal, Canada; Professor Amani K. Hamdan Alghamdi, Imam Abdulrahman Bin Faisal University, Dammam, Saudi Arabia; National Down Syndrome Society, United States; Kevin Noh, Canada; Shokan Omarov, First Secretary, Embassy of Kazakhstan in Canada; Katherine Rodriguez, Costa Rica; and the Uganda National Association of the Deaf and the Good Samaritan School for the Deaf, Uganda. I am especially grateful to Alisa Baldwin, Karen Boersma, Sophie Casson, Karen Li, Stacey Roderick, Debbie Rogosin, Jennifer Stokes, and Niki Walker for their valuable contributions in bringing this book to life!

ONTARIO ARTS COUNCIL
CONSEIL DES ARTS DE L'ONTARIO
an Ontario government agency
un organisme du gouvernement de l'Ontario

Canada Council
for the Arts
Conseil des Arts
du Canada

Canadä

Publisher of Chirp, Chickadee and OWL
www.owlkidsbooks.com

Owlkids Books is a division of bayard canada

Owlkids Books acknowledges the financial support of the Canada Council for the Arts, the Ontario Arts Council, the Government of Canada through the Canada Book Fund (CBF), and the Government of Ontario through the Ontario Creates Book Initiative for our publishing activities.

Published in Canada by Owlkids Books Inc.
1 Eglinton Avenue East, Toronto, ON, M4P 3A1

Published in the US by Owlkids Books Inc.
1700 Fourth Street, Berkeley, CA, 94710

Library of Congress Control Number:
2021930825

Library and Archives Canada Cataloguing in Publication

Title: Same here! : the differences we share / written by Susan Hughes ; illustrated by Sophie Casson.
Names: Hughes, Susan, 1960- author. Casson, Sophie, illustrator.
Identifiers: Canadiana 20210267593 ISBN 9781771473071 (hardcover)
Subjects: LCSH: Children—Cross-cultural studies—Juvenile literature.
Classification: LCC GN482 .H84 2022 DDC j305.23—dc23

Edited by Karen Li
Designed by Alisa Baldwin

MIX
Paper from
responsible sources
FSC® C104723

Manufactured in Guangdong Province, Dongguan City, China, in October 2021, by Toppan Leefung Packaging & Printing (Dongguan) Co., Ltd.   Job #BAYDC96

A   B   C   D   E   F